Soccer
LEGENDS

Blaine Wiseman

AV² provides enriched content that supplements and complements this book. Weigl's AV² books strive to create inspired learning and engage young minds in a total learning experience.

Your AV² Media Enhanced books come alive with...

Audio
Listen to sections of the book read aloud.

Key Words
Study vocabulary, and complete a matching word activity.

Video
Watch informative video clips.

Quizzes
Test your knowledge.

Embedded Weblinks
Gain additional information for research.

Slide Show
View images and captions, and prepare a presentation.

Try This!
Complete activities and hands-on experiments.

... and much, much more!

Go to **www.av2books.com**, and enter this book's unique code.

BOOK CODE

Q 5 8 4 7 9 7

AV² by Weigl brings you media enhanced books that support active learning.

Published by AV² by Weigl
350 5th Avenue, 59th Floor
New York, NY 10118
Website: www.av2books.com

Library of Congress Control Number: 2016956745

ISBN 978-1-4896-5269-0 (hardcover)
ISBN 978-1-4896-5270-6 (softcover)
ISBN 978-1-4896-5271-3 (multi-user eBook)

Printed in the United States of America, in Brainerd, Minnesota
1 2 3 4 5 6 7 8 9 20 19 18 17 16

122016
113016

Project Coordinator: Jared Siemens
Designer: Terry Paulhus

Photo Credits
Every reasonable effort has been made to trace ownership and to obtain permission to reprint copyright material. The publisher would be pleased to have any errors or omissions brought to their attention so that they may be corrected in subsequent printings. The publisher acknowledges Getty Images, iStock, and Alamy as its primary image suppliers for this title.

Soccer
LEGENDS

Contents

History and Culture

The game of soccer has been played all over the world for centuries. Outside the United States, Canada, and Australia, soccer is called football. It was first played in Great Britain in the 1800s. Later, the sport spread to other parts of the world, such as Africa, the Caribbean, and South America. Countries in these regions have become known for their excellent soccer players. Today, soccer has more players and **spectators** than any other sport. The sport is governed by an organization called the Fédération Internacionale de Football Association (FIFA).

Argentinian Lionel Messi is often considered one of the best soccer players of all time. He has been named FIFA World Player of the Year a record five times.

Organized soccer has had a long history in the United Kingdom. Today, there are long-standing, fierce rivalries between national teams, such as England and Scotland.

Swapping Jerseys

After a soccer match, players on opposite teams often trade jerseys with each other. This tradition began in 1931, when France's team asked England's team for their jerseys. France had beaten England for the first time, and wanted to show their respect for a well-played game. Even though players are fiercely competitive during a game, swapping jerseys afterward shows that they appreciate their opponent's hard work.

UEFA Champions League Anthem

One of the biggest competitions in European soccer is the Union of European Football Association's (UEFA) Champions League. The UEFA was created to make soccer games more **professional**. It added more teams to the league, more locations for the games, and has higher standards for how fans behave at the games. Before each Champions League game, the UEFA Champions League anthem is played. The anthem was created in 1992 and has lyrics in English, French, and German. The anthem has become a symbol of soccer's best games and the world's best players. It is a signal that world-class soccer is about to be played.

Soccer Scarves

Soccer scarves are one of the most visible traditions among fans. Before a match, fans often create a "wall" with their scarves by holding them in the air while singing their national anthem. The tradition of using scarves began in the early 1900s, when British soccer fans wore them to stay warm at matches. Today, scarves carry a team's colors and crest. Waving them in the stands has become a much-loved tradition.

The World Cup

Germany won the most recent FIFA World Cup in 2014. From the beginning, Germany was considered to be the best team in the tournament. The team was led by young, high-power players Mario Göetze, André Schürrle, and Jérôme Boateng.

The FIFA World Cup and the FIFA Women's World Cup are the best-known soccer tournaments in the world. More people watch this tournament's final game than any other single sporting event. In 2015, more than 750 million television viewers watched the FIFA Women's World Cup.

The World Cup has been held every four years since it began in 1930, except during World War II. The Women's World Cup began in 1991. FIFA is made up of 208 men's and 177 women's national soccer teams. Over the four years leading up to each World Cup, those teams compete for a spot in the final. In total, 32 teams for men and 24 for women compete in the World Cup, which has several rounds. Some rounds are single **elimination**, while others are not. The winning team from the final round wins the World Cup trophy.

The World Cup trophy used today was designed in 1974 by Silvio Gazzaniga of Italy. It shows two players celebrating victory, holding the world over their heads. Each winning team takes home a replica of the trophy. The original is locked away after the winning match for safe keeping.

WORLD CUP RECORDS

227 POINTS — Brazil holds the record for the most **all-time World Cup points.**

12 GOALS — The **most goals** ever scored in a single game was in 1954, when Austria played Switzerland.

3 WINS — In women's World Cup soccer, the United States has **more wins** than any other country.

25 MATCHES — Lothar Matthaeus from Germany holds the record for the **most matches played** in the World Cup.

17 YEARS OLD — The **youngest player** to compete in the World Cup was Norman Whiteside of Northern Ireland in 1982.

Jules Rimet Cup

From 1930 to 1974, the Jules Rimet Cup was the World Cup trophy. It was named after Jules Rimet, who organized the first World Cup tournament. During World War II, FIFA's vice president hid the Jules Rimet Cup under his bed. In 1966, the cup was stolen and later found in Great Britain. The cup was retired in 1970, after Brazil won it for a third time. The cup was stolen from Rio de Janeiro in 1983, and some people believe it was melted for its gold.

WORLD CUP WINNERS

 Brazil . . . .  **5**

 Italy . . . .  **4**

 Germany **4**

 Uruguay **2**

Argentina **2**

Soccer Equipment

Soccer equipment is simple. Players only need a ball, a field, and two goals, which are the nets on either end of the field. During each 90-minute game, players kick the soccer ball across the field, or pitch, and try to send it into the opposing team's goal.

JERSEYS

Soccer jerseys are used to tell teams and players apart on the field. Goalkeepers wear a different color of jersey than the other players. This makes them easier for the referee to spot. Players have their name and number on the back of their jersey, and their team's logo on the front.

The color of a jersey almost always corresponds with a team's colors. During his time with AC Milan, David Beckham wore the team colors of black and red.

When players represent their home country on national teams, their uniform colors usually reflect their national flag colors. Goalkeeper Hope Solo has worn red, white, and blue while representing the United States.

SOCCER BALL

Soccer balls are specially designed to fly through the air at fast speeds. Players kick the ball in different ways to make it spin, rise, or drop in midair. Soccer balls have 32 black and white panels, and are made from **synthetic** materials. A regulation soccer ball is 27 to 28 inches (69 to 71 centimeters) around.

SHIN GUARDS

Players are required to wear shin guards for protection. Soccer is a contact sport, so there is always a risk of being kicked. Shin guards are made from lightweight yet strong materials, such as fiberglass, foam, or plastic.

CLEATS

Soccer shoes have small bumps or blades called cleats attached to the bottom of the shoe. The cleats sink into the field's surface. This provides better traction for the players, even when the ground is wet or muddy. Soccer shoes that are used for indoor soccer are made with softer, more flexible bumps, or have no cleats at all.

Greatest Legends

With its giant fan base, professional soccer has created a huge culture around its star players. Fans love to debate who the best player is, whether in the past or in the present. It can be hard to judge who is the best, since players have skills in different positions. However, a few soccer players have become true legends.

Pelé

Pelé is one of the best-known soccer players in history. Born Edson Arantes do Nascimento, he was given the nickname Pelé, which means "miracle" in **Hebrew**. People all over the world enjoyed watching Pelé play. It is rumored that in 1969, Pelé played a game in Nigeria, where a war was taking place. The two sides called a **cease-fire** so they could watch Pelé play. In 1999, FIFA named Pelé co-Player of the Century, along with Diego Maradona of Argentina.

Mia Hamm

Mia Hamm is considered the best women's soccer player in history. As a member of the U.S. women's national soccer team, she won two Women's World Cup titles and two Olympic gold medals over the course of 17 years. Hamm won her first Women's World Cup title when she was 19 years old. During her career, Hamm gained a huge number of fans and became a U.S. icon. She was named FIFA Women's World Player of the Year in 2001, and again in 2002.

Most Women's World Cup Matches Played

Even though the Women's World Cup is newer than the Men's, some women have played in an impressive number of matches. These five women hold records for the most World Cup matches played.

1st	Abby Wambach	32
2nd	Kristin Lilly	30
2nd	Homare Sawa	30
3rd	Formiga	27
4th	Carli Lloyd	25

Lev Yashin

Lev Yashin played for Dinamo Moscow, in Russia, from 1953 until 1971. He is considered to be the greatest goalkeeper in soccer history. Yashin was called the "Black Spider" because of his black uniform and amazing speed and skill when blocking shots. Yashin played internationally for the **Soviet Union**. He won the 1956 Olympic gold medal and the 1960 European Championship. Yashin is the only goalkeeper ever to win the FIFA European Player of the Year Award.

Top U.S. Scorers

Goals are scored when the ball passes into the zone surrounded by the net. Each goal is worth one point. Over the course of their careers, these players have scored the most goals for the U.S. national teams.

MEN	GOALS
Landon Donovan	57
Clint Dempsey	48
Eric Wynalda	34
Brian McBride	30
Jozy Altidore	29

WOMEN	GOALS
Abby Wambach	184
Mia Hamm	158
Kristine Lilly	130
Michelle Akers	107
Tiffeny Milbrett	100

Carli Lloyd is a two-time U.S. Olympic gold medalist. She was voted FIFA World Player of the Year and U.S. Soccer Player of the Year in 2015.

Playing the Field

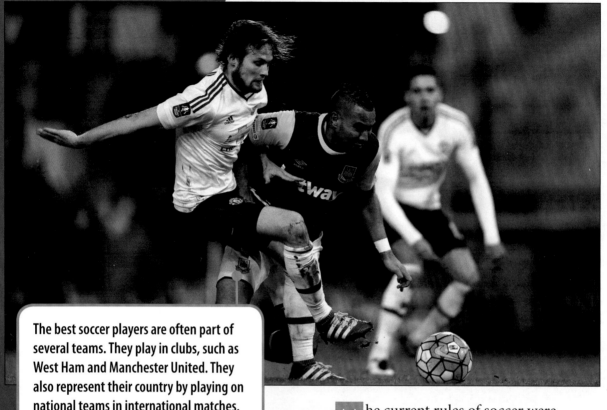

The best soccer players are often part of several teams. They play in clubs, such as West Ham and Manchester United. They also represent their country by playing on national teams in international matches.

The current rules of soccer were developed in Great Britain in 1863. They are called the Cambridge Rules. The different positions in soccer were first established with the modern game. In today's game, each team has 10 fielders and 1 goalkeeper. The fielders are split into defenders, midfielders, and forwards. Each team member has a specific job as they try to score goals while defending their own net. Goalkeepers are allowed to stop the ball with their hands. However, other soccer players are not typically allowed to touch the ball with their hands. They use their feet, legs, and heads to score goals.

Before his retirement in 2015, Nigeria's national goalkeeper Vincent Enyeama represented his country in four World Cups. He had the most international game appearances for Nigeria, with 101.

Goal-Scoring Goalkeepers

On rare occasions, goalkeepers score goals for their team. This can happen through **free kicks** and **penalties**. These three goalkeepers have scored the most goals.

PLAYER	GOALS
Rogerio Ceni	129
Jose Luis Chilavert	62
Dimitar Ivankov	42

Top-Scoring Men in the World Cup

Soccer games often have very low scores. Most matches are won with fewer than five points scored. These are the highest scorers in a single game during the World Cup.

PLAYER	POINTS
Oleg Salenko	5
Just Fontaine	4
Sandor Kocsis	4
Ademir Marques de Menezes	4
Ernest Wilimowski	4

Most World Cup Assists

An assist is when a team member passes the ball to another player, who then scores. Soccer players consider assists an important part of scoring. These players have tied for the most assists in a single World Cup game.

PLAYER	ASSISTS
Thomas Muller	4
Bastian Schweinsteiger	4
Juan Cuadrado	4
Lionel Messi	4

Oldest World Cup Players

43	Faryd Mondragón
42	Roger Milla
41	Pat Jennings
40	Peter Shilton
40	Dino Zoff

Columbian goalie Faryd Mondragón became the oldest player to play in a World Cup match during round three of the 2014 FIFA World Cup. In 1930, at the first World Cup, more than half the players were age 24 or younger. Today, the average age of a player is 27.4.

Money Makers

Soccer teams are businesses. People all over the world pay to see their favorite teams compete. In addition, teams and international soccer organizations make money through advertising and by selling tickets to fans. Companies even sponsor individual players to advertise their products. Soccer has become a global **industry**. An average fan will spend about $80 when going to a match.

SOFT DRINK
$3.50

HOT DOG
$3.50

TICKET
$46.22

SCARF
$20.00

TOTAL
$78.22

Business of Soccer

People pay billions of dollars to own soccer teams. These teams can make large amounts of money for their owners. The top five most valuable soccer teams are all owned by individuals or families.

$3.5 BILLION
FC Barcelona

$3.3 BILLION
Manchester United

$3.26 BILLION
Real Madrid

$2.6 BILLION
Bayern Munich

$2 BILLION
Arsenal

Sponsorships

Sponsorships are essential to the financial success of soccer. Teams and players make money by having companies sponsor them. Sponsoring companies often have their name or logo displayed on the team jersey or stadium. Some of the biggest soccer sponsors are Adidas, Nike, and Chevrolet.

Sporting Salaries

Some professional soccer players earn millions of dollars. A portion of that money comes from sponsorships, but many also receive large salaries. These athletes are currently paid the most money for their sport annually.

Lionel Messi
$77 million

Cristiano Ronaldo
$82 million

Garth Bale
$34 million

Neymar Jr
$36 million

Zlatan Ibrahimovic
$37 million

Soccer Stadiums of the World

Arctic Ocean

Soccer is a sport full of history and tradition. Many teams have played on the same grounds for more than 100 years. For players and fans alike, stadiums take on special meaning. Each stadium is unique in location, traditions, features, and history. This map shows some of the best-known soccer stadiums around the world.

NORTH AMERICA

Pacific Ocean

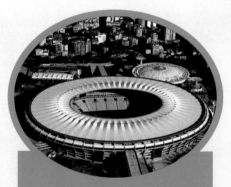

THE AZADI STADIUM
Tehran, Iran

The Azadi Stadium is one of the most impressive soccer stadiums in the world. Located in Iran, the stadium can seat nearly 90,000 fans. It also includes training facilities separate from the main field.

THE MARACANA
Rio de Janeiro, Brazil

The Maracana is the largest soccer stadium in Brazil and the second largest in South America. It has a seating capacity of 78,838.

SOUTH AMERICA

Atlant Ocea

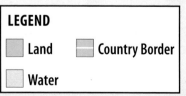

LEGEND
- Land
- Water
- Country Border

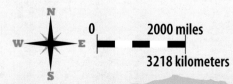

N
W E
S

0   2000 miles

3218 kilometers

Arctic Ocean

BRAMALL LANE
Sheffield, Great Britain

Bramall Lane is the oldest soccer stadium in the world. It opened in England in 1855, around the time modern soccer first developed.

EUROPE

ASIA

Pacific Ocean

AFRICA

Indian Ocean

WEMBLEY STADIUM
London, Great Britain

Wembley Stadium cost more than $1.2 billion to build. It is the fourth most expensive soccer stadium in the world. It seats 90,000 fans and hosted soccer during the 2012 Olympics.

Southern Ocean

ANTARCTICA

Coaches and Officials

When soccer games run smoothly, it is often thanks to coaches and referees. Coaches work with teams throughout the season to help them build skills and strategies. During a game, the coach will offer advice to his or her team. Head coaches are often called managers.

Referees are on the field while games are being played. Their main job is to call fouls when a player breaks one of the rules of the game. Referees also keep time and signal when a ball has gone out of bounds. They are neutral in the game, taking neither team's side.

Sir Alex Ferguson

One of the most successful soccer managers in history is Sir Alex Ferguson, who coached Manchester United. Ferguson first coached in a soccer league called the Scottish Premier League. In 1986, he moved to Manchester, where he led the team to 13 league titles. In total, he won 49 trophies as a coach, more than any other in Great Britain.

Sir Alex Ferguson's Top Tournament Wins

5	Football Association Challenge Cups
10	Community Shields
4	English Football League Cups
2	Union of European Football Associations Champions League
1	World Club Cup

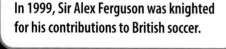

In 1999, Sir Alex Ferguson was knighted for his contributions to British soccer.

Luis Enrique was one of Spain's greatest players before his retirement in 2004. Since then, he has coached in Spain and Italy. He is now the manager of FC Barcelona.

Leading the Charge

Many soccer coaches are former professional players. Some of them were legends while on the field. These coaches have earned the most points over their playing careers.

COACH	POINTS
Luis Enrique, Barcelona	20,596
Unai Emery, Sevill	13,468
Josep "Pep" Guardiola, Bayern München	13,350

Most Finishes in the World Cup Top Four

Some coaches were talented enough to coach in multiple World Cup tournaments. These coaches led their teams to more than one finish in the top four.

COACH	FINISHES
Helmut Schön, West Germany	3
Mário Zagallo, Brazil	3
Luiz Felipe Scolari, Brazil and Portugal	3

Rinus Michels

Rinus Michels, from the Netherlands, is one of the best coaches in history. He coached from 1960 to 1992. As a coach, he built champion soccer clubs with Ajax, FC Köln, Barcelona, and Bayer Leverkusen. In 1999, FIFA named him the manager of the century.

Between 1964 and 1978, Helmut Schön managed the West German national team. Under his leadership, West Germany appeared in many international tournaments and won the 1974 FIFA World Cup.

Most Valuable Players

Each year, the representatives of the media award one soccer player the Adidas Golden Ball award, along with the title of Most Valuable Player (MVP). The MVP is the player that has been the biggest value to his team. Whether the player has already been an MVP in the past and the number of games he or she played during the season is also taken into consideration. Being named MVP is known as "winning the Golden Ball." These players have all been recent MVPs.

Lionel Messi

2014 MVP • FORWARD • ARGENTINA

Lionel Messi was born in Argentina in 1987. At age 13, he moved to Spain to play for FC Barcelona. Messi quickly became a star in Spain. He scored four goals for Argentina during the 2014 FIFA World Cup. Though his team lost in the finals, he was still awarded the Adidas Golden Ball for his efforts.

Diego Forlán

2010 MVP • FORWARD • URUGUAY

Diego Forlán was born in Uruguay, and he has played for clubs all over the world. Forlán was an essential member of Uruguay's team in the 2010 World Cup. He was also tied for the top scorer in that year's tournament. He holds Uruguay's record for the most international appearances.

Zinedine Zidane

2006 MVP • MIDFIELDER • FRANCE

Zinedine Zidane is considered an all-time great in the soccer world. The French player was named FIFA World Player of the Year three times. In 1998, he helped France win the World Cup. During the 2006 World Cup finals, he scored a goal during a penalty kick, which secured his MVP status.

Carli Lloyd

2015 MVP • MIDFIELDER • UNITED STATES

Carli Lloyd was born in New Jersey in 1982. Lloyd joined the U.S. senior team as a center midfielder in 2005. In 2007, she played in her first FIFA Women's World Cup. In 2015, during her third World Cup, Lloyd scored twice within the first five minutes of the championship game against Japan. Within 16 minutes, she had scored three times, securing her MVP status. She was awarded the Golden Ball after the U.S. won the 2015 FIFA Women's World Cup.

Homare Sawa

2011 MVP • MIDFIELDER • JAPAN

Sawa Homare was born in Tokyo in 1978. By the time she was 15, she was playing for Japan's national team. Homare attended every World Cup between 1995 and 2015. In 2011, she led Japan to the World Cup Finals, where she scored the tying goal in overtime against the United States. That year, Japan won the 2011 FIFA Women's World Cup. Homare was awarded the Golden Ball for her efforts in the finals, and she was later named FIFA's 2011 Player of the Year. She retired in 2015.

Marta Vieira da Silva

2007 MVP • FORWARD • BRAZIL

Marta Vieira da Silva, simply known as Marta, was born in 1986 in Dois Riachos, Brazil. Marta was discouraged from playing soccer for most of her childhood because she was a girl. When she was 14, she was discovered by a scout looking to begin a women's team. In 2003, she played for Brazil in her first FIFA Women's World Cup. She scored three goals during the tournament. In 2007, Brazil made it to the finals, and Marta led the team to a second-place finish. She scored seven goals during the tournament and secured the Golden Ball. Marta has been named FIFA World Player of the Year five times.

Quiz

Now that you have read about soccer legends, test your knowledge by answering these questions. All of the information can be found in the text. The answers are also provided for reference.

1 Where did modern soccer begin?

A: Great Britain

2 What is the international governing body for soccer?

A: FIFA

3 What items do soccer players often swap at the end of the game?

A: Jerseys

4 What is the best-known international soccer tournament?

A: FIFA World Cup

5 Which country has won the most World Cup titles?

A: Brazil

6 Which well-known soccer player has a nickname that means "miracle" in Hebrew?

A: Pelé

7 Which female soccer player led her team to a Women's World Cup title at age 19?

A: Mia Hamm

8 What is the world's oldest soccer stadium?

A: Bramall Lane

Key Words

cease-fire: an agreement between two groups to stop fighting

elimination: the process of getting rid of something

free kicks: the act of allowing players to kick the ball without pressure from the other team

Hebrew: Jewish language and culture

industry: an activity that generates a product for money

penalties: free kicks from a place on the field that is in front of the goal; the goalkeeper must defend the net without the help of other team members

professional: paid to participate in a sport or activity

Soviet Union: a former group of countries in Eastern Europe with Moscow as its capital

spectators: people who watch a show or game

synthetic: a human-made product that is similar to a product found in nature

Index

Log on to www.av2books.com

AV² by Weigl brings you media enhanced books that support active learning. Go to www.av2books.com, and enter the special code found on page 2 of this book. You will gain access to enriched and enhanced content that supplements and complements this book. Content includes video, audio, weblinks, quizzes, a slide show, and activities.

AV² Online Navigation

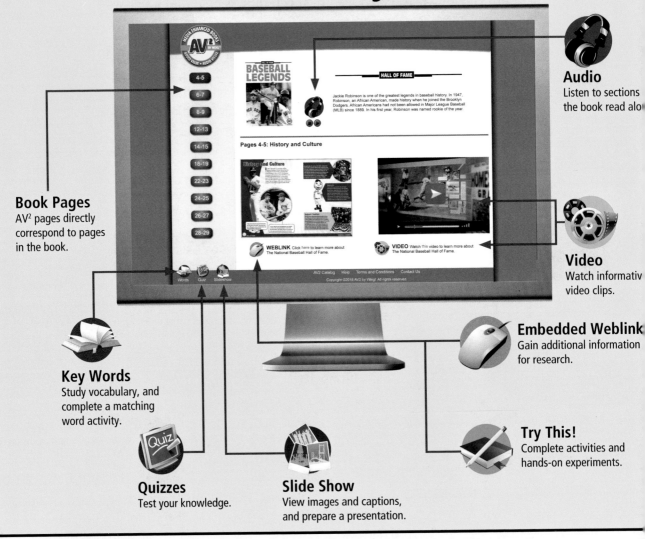

Audio
Listen to sections the book read alo

Book Pages
AV² pages directly correspond to pages in the book.

Video
Watch informativ video clips.

Key Words
Study vocabulary, and complete a matching word activity.

Embedded Weblink
Gain additional information for research.

Quizzes
Test your knowledge.

Slide Show
View images and captions, and prepare a presentation.

Try This!
Complete activities and hands-on experiments.

AV² was built to bridge the gap between print and digital. We encourage you to tell us what you like and what you want to see in the future.

Sign up to be an AV² Ambassador at www.av2books.com/ambassador.

Due to the dynamic nature of the Internet, some of the URLs and activities provided as part of AV² by Weigl may have changed or ceased to exist. AV² by Weigl accepts no responsibility for any such changes. All media enhanced books are regularly monitored to update addresses and sites in a timely manner. Contact AV² by Weigl at 1-866-649-3445 or av2books@weigl.com with any questions, comments, or feedback.